The Missions of California

Mission Santa Bárbara

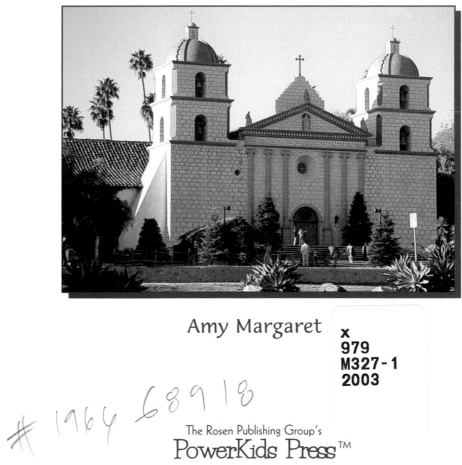

Amy Margaret

The Rosen Publishing Group's
PowerKids Press™
New York

To Cowboy Dan and his Queen

Published in 2000, 2003 by The Rosen Publishing Group, Inc.
29 East 21st Street, New York, NY 10010

Photo Credits and Photo Illustrations: pp. 1, 17, 26, 28, 31, 33, 36, 43, 47, 50 by Cristina Taccone; pp. 4, 35, 48, 49 © Shirley Jordan; p. 6 © The Bridgeman Art Library International Ltd.; p. 7 © North Wind Picture Archives; pp. 8, 12, 39, 40, 42 © Michael K. Ward; p. 9 © CORBIS/Bettmann; p.11 by Santa Barbara Historical Society; pp. 14, 25, 32 © Gil Cohen; p. 16 © CORBIS/Richard Cummins; pp. 22, 29, 45 © Department of Special Collections, University of Southern California Libraries; pp. 18, 26 by Tim Hall; pp. 20, 24 © Seaver Center for Western History Research, L.A. County Museum of Natural History; pp. 23, 34, 37 © Eda Rogers; pp. 35, 46 © The Bancroft Library; p. 50 © Ernest H. Rogers, pp. 52, 57 by Christine Innamorato.

Revised Edition 2003

Book Design: Danielle Primiceri
Layout: Felicity Erwin

Editorial Consultant Coordinator: Karen Fontanetta, M.A., Curator, Mission San Miguel Arcángel
Editorial Consultant: Kristina Foss, Director, Santa Bárbara Mission Museum
Historical Photo Consultants: Thomas L. Davis, M. Div., M.A.
                                        Michael K. Ward, M.A.

Margaret, Amy.
        Mission Santa Bárbara / by Amy Margaret. — 1st ed.
            p.   cm. — (The missions of California)
        Includes bibliographical references (p. 62) and index.
        Summary: Discusses the Mission Santa Bárbara from its founding in 1786 to the present day, including the reasons for Spanish colonization in California and the effects of colonization on the Chumash Indians.
        ISBN 0-8239-5880-9 (lib. bdg.)
        1. Santa Bárbara Mission Juvenile literature. 2. Spanish mission buildings—California—Santa Barbara Region—History Juvenile literature. 3. Franciscans—California—Santa Barbara Region—History Juvenile literature. 4. Chumash Indians—Missions—California—Santa Barbara Region—History Juvenile literature. 5. California—History—To 1846 Juvenile literature. [1. Santa Bárbara Mission—History. 2. Missions—California. 3. Chumash Indians—Missions. 4. Indians of North America—Missions—California. 5. California—History—To 1846.] I. Title. II. Series.
        F869.S45M37   1999
        979.4'91—dc21   99-27379
                                                                                              CIP

Manufactured in the United States of America

Contents

Spain Explores America

In Southern California, about 90 miles (145 km) north of the bustling city of Los Angeles, is the town of Santa Barbara. Many of its streets are lined with palm trees, and all along the city's beach is a boardwalk, perfect for in-line skating, bicycling, or just strolling. Overlooking the beautiful area on a hill is Mission Santa Bárbara, which today serves as a church, museum, and a favorite visitor spot. More than 200 years ago, Mission Santa Bárbara served a different purpose. It was home to Spanish missionaries, soldiers, and the Chumash Indians.

In the 1500s, the Spanish first learned about the rich, fertile land of North America and the various American Indian tribes that lived there. In the 1700s, they became eager to settle the land and create a mission system. A mission is a place where people gather to learn about a certain religion. Sometimes people live in a mission and learn a trade. Spanish explorers sailed up the coast of California looking for places to start missions. Eventually they built a chain of 21 missions up the coast of California. Spain's main objective was to teach the Indians about Christianity so that they could become Spanish citizens, thus expanding Spain's empire throughout California.

The scenic area near today's city of Santa Barbara is home to one of the most beautiful Spanish missions. Mission Santa Bárbara, the 10th mission founded, was built in 1786, almost 20 years after the founding of the first mission. Initial plans for exploring the New World (North America, South America, and Central America) actually began more than 200 years earlier in Spain.

Many people come to visit Mission Santa Bárbara today.

5

King Ferdinand and Queen Isabella of Spain commissioned Columbus to find new trade routes to Asia.

California's First Explorers

During the 1400s, many people thought that the world was flat. Nobody knew exactly how much more land there was to be conquered. European explorers set out to find riches and land that would make their own countries wealthier. Spain had some of the most aggressive explorers in all of Europe.

In 1492, King Ferdinand and Queen Isabella of Spain sent Christopher Columbus to find Asia. Columbus decided to sail west. He discovered today's West Indies, below the state of Florida.

A string of explorers followed, including Ferdinand Magellan, who led an expedition that proved the earth was round by sailing all the way around the world. Juan Rodríguez Cabrillo and Sebastián Vizcaíno were two other brave men who set out from Spain to explore the so-called New World.

Juan Rodríguez Cabrillo

In 1542, the viceroy of New Spain sent Juan Rodríguez Cabrillo to explore the western coast of North America. Today the area of New Spain is the country of Mexico. New Spain at that time belonged to Spain, and the viceroy ruled over New Spain as a representative of the king of Spain. Cabrillo's instructions were to find a waterway that would join the Pacific and Atlantic Oceans. He and his crew were also supposed to look for harbors, where Spanish ships could rest on their long voyages. They sailed from New Spain up the coast of Baja, or lower, California and into Alta, or upper, California. Today Alta California is part of the state of California and Baja California is now called the Baja Peninsula and is part of Mexico. When Cabrillo explored California, he claimed these coastal lands for Spain.

Spanish ships sailed along the Pacific Coast looking for harbors and rivers.

Cabrillo and his men sailed up the coast. Although they didn't know it at the time, the explorers were seeing several future mission sites, including the sites where Mission San Diego de Alcalá, Mission Santa Bárbara, and Mission San Carlos Borromeo de Carmelo would be built. They even came in contact with California Indians who gave them food.

The ships sailed as far north as what is today the state of Oregon.

The expedition proved that Alta California was a large mainland, not an island. Cabrillo died on the voyage, but he is still considered one of the first explorers of the California coast. He and his crew laid the foundation for future expeditions to Alta California.

Sebastián Vizcaíno

Spanish explorer Sebastián Vizcaíno's first encounter with California Indians was in 1602, when he witnessed a boat similar to a canoe gliding swiftly in the water just inside the Santa Barbara Channel. Vizcaíno ordered his men to give the Indians cloth and food. The California Indians gave the Spanish explorers fish to eat. Vizcaíno and his crew were impressed with these friendly, quiet people, who were called the Chumash Indians.

Like Cabrillo, Vizcaíno had been sent by ship to find a connecting waterway between the Atlantic and Pacific Oceans. Vizcaíno and his ships sailed northward and came upon a safe harbor. Vizcaíno named it Monterey, after the viceroy of New Spain.

Like his predecessor, Vizcaíno was unable to find a passageway connecting the Atlantic and Pacific Oceans. There is a passageway north of North America, but it is frozen most of the year. The Spanish explorers didn't go that far north because their ships couldn't sail through the icy waters. When Vizcaíno told the viceroy about his journey, the viceroy deemed it to be unsuccessful since the goal of finding the passageway had not been met. The viceroy did not believe that the trips were worth the time and money needed to finance them. Spanish rule was maintained in New Spain, but no further explorations went up the coast to Alta California for the next 160 years.

In the meantime, Russian and English rulers had heard rumors of the great land that Spain had found. Both countries started sending ships to the western coast. Spain became concerned that they would lose the land that Cabrillo and Vizcaíno had already claimed, so they quickly took measures to permanently control the California land.

Vizcaíno and his men had to find shelter from a storm on December 4, 1602. December 4 is the feast of Saint Barbara. So Vizcaíno named the area for Saint Barbara.

The Chumash

Before European explorers visited new lands across the Atlantic Ocean, American Indians had been living in the California area for thousands of years. When Vizcaíno visited Alta California, more than 300,000 American Indians lived on this land. The Indians lived in villages of around 80 to 100 people belonging to the same tribe. Different tribes had different areas of land they considered their own.

Over 40 Chumash villages lay along the coast near where Mission Santa Bárbara would be founded. There were another 15 villages on the islands nearby. In California there were more Chumash Indians than any other American Indian tribe.

The Chumash Village

The Chumash built homes that were dome-shaped and could hold as many as 50 people. The buildings in the village were covered with mats of tule, which were tightly woven reeds used to keep out the wind and rain.

Every village had at least one *temescal*, or sweat lodge. Men used the *temescal* before special religious ceremonies or hunting trips. Sometimes the *temescal* was a place of social gathering or a work area. Occasionally women used it. The Indians would sit naked in a small room in front of a blazing fire. These rooms were similar to today's saunas or steam rooms. After sweating and cleansing their bodies, they would run into the ocean or nearby lake or stream. This method was also believed to cure many illnesses.

The highest population of Indians in California was found in the Santa ▶ Barbara Channel area.

The Chumash People

A chief and a shaman led every Chumash village. The chief was in charge of passing out food and valuables to the tribe members. He was also the leader in battles with other tribes. The biggest disputes were usually over control of land for hunting or gathering food.

The shaman was the religious leader of the village. The shaman guided those who were sick and was also called on to find new food sources or, in some cases, to try to bring rain. Although men usually served in the chief and shaman positions, women held these leadership roles, too.

The Chumash spent most days hunting, gathering, and preparing food. The women gathered fruits, nuts, herbs, and vegetables from bushes and trees. After picking acorns and finding seeds, the Chumash women ground it into flour. The men, who were usually naked, hunted for food such as fish and small animals. When it was colder, they wore coats that reached their waists. The village chiefs could be distinguished by their longer cloaks that hung to their ankles. Women wore skirts made of antelope hide or deerskin that reached to their knees.

Shamans sometimes wore decorative costumes.

The Chumash were known throughout the land for building the strongest and quickest boats. Similar to canoes, these boats were called *tomols*. The Chumash used the *tomols* for fishing and for traveling to nearby islands. One *tomol* could easily hold up to 10 people. The Chumash caught a variety of fish and sharks from the Pacific Ocean. The Chumash were surrounded by plenty of food sources and had no need to plant and farm. They survived by living off the land.

Older tribespeople taught the young children in the village the skills they would need as they grew into adulthood. Boys were taught to hunt and make tools. Girls learned to weave baskets and to gather and prepare food.

The Chumash Tradition

While all members of Chumash villages worked hard, they also had time for recreation. Most villages had a specific area for playing games and holding dances. One game was called hoop and pole. The object of the game was to throw a long pole through a hoop.

The Chumash performed ritualistic dances for celebrations and ceremonies. They also danced as a way of giving thanks to the earth for providing for their needs. The Chumash Indians believed that gods could be found in people, birds, animals, fish, and all living things. They respected the land by hunting and gathering only what they needed to live. Some historians think that the Chumash worshiped the sun and moon as gods and believed in good and evil spirits.

The Chumash had everything they needed to continue to be a thriving people for centuries. While some Chumash descendants still survive today, the Spanish influence on their way of life destroyed the traditional Chumash heritage that existed for generations. The Chumash way of life was forever changed by the arrival of the Spanish and the establishment of Mission Santa Bárbara.

The Mission System and Its Founders

Many years before the founding of Mission Santa Bárbara, the Spanish first settled in New Spain. During the 1500s, they established a capital in Mexico City and built missions throughout the region. In 1573, the government of New Spain passed the Law of the Indies, which said that Spain's main goal in New Spain was to convert the Indians to Christianity and to expand the size of the Spanish empire.

The Spanish felt strongly that the Indians living in New Spain should adopt their Christian religion, language, and lifestyle. They viewed the Indians as "uncivilized" because the Indians lived their lives so differently from the Europeans. The Indians were not educated in schools, they wore little clothing, and they lived off the land. They thought it was best for the Indians to adopt Spanish customs and to believe in the Christian faith. The Spanish believed they were helping to save the Indians' souls by converting them from their "primitive" way of life to what they believed was the proper Christian way. The Spanish believed that the Indians would learn to appreciate the Spanish culture, religion, and manufactured goods and think of Spanish ideas and objects as superior to what they had known and used before. The Spanish held these beliefs largely because of the cultural isolation of the time. This way of thinking led to the destruction of many California Indian groups and their interesting and diverse cultures.

The Spanish government had procedures for building the missions in New Spain. Soldiers and missionaries were sent to teach the Indians about Christianity. Using the labor of the Indians, the Spanish built *presidios*, or forts, where the military soldiers were stationed. Each *presidio's* function was to protect its inhabitants from outside attackers

The Chumash were converted to Christianity in a ceremony
◀ *called baptism. After being baptized, the Indians were*
no longer allowed to practice their old religion.

and to stop any Indian revolts or civil problems. Missionaries taught the Indians how to grow food, raise cattle, and make tools and goods such as soap, candles, horseshoes, and leather and woven goods. Having the Indians learn trades would help the economy of the missions. The Spanish believed that once the Indians learned how to grow their food, instead of hunting for it, they could live in permanent Spanish villages.

The Spanish believed it would take about 10 years to train the Indians so that they could be self-sufficient

▲
Santa Barbara was the site of one of the four Spanish presidios, which protected the mission and Spain's claim to the lands of Alta California.

and live on their own in their new environment. Once the missionaries felt that the Indians were ready for this, the mission land would be returned to them and the Indians would be expected to operate them as tax-paying

Spanish citizens. This process is called secularization. The missionaries would then leave and travel to new areas to establish new missions and convert more Indians, thus expanding the Spanish empire. Although the California missions did end up becoming secularized, it did not happen according to the Spanish plan.

By the mid-1700s, the Spanish had many missions set up and running in what we now call Central and South America, as well as in what is today Mexico. After learning about the English and Russian explorers, the Spanish knew that they had to work fast at establishing missions in Alta California to maintain their control over this land.

Junípero Serra

When plans to build missions in Alta California began, one man stood out from the others as the one to bring the Christian faith to the Indians and lead the other Spanish missionaries.

Fray Junípero Serra was the founder of the first nine California missions and had set in motion the founding of Mission Santa Bárbara before his death in 1784. He was in his mid-50s when he founded the first mission in what is today the area of San Diego. Serra had been working toward this goal for most of his life, since he was a young teenager.

▲
Saint Francis of Assisi founded the Franciscan order.

Born Miguel José in November of 1713, the future missionary devoted his entire life to the Catholic faith. He was educated by Franciscans, who are members of a Catholic order of friars. They were called Franciscans because they lived by the Christian example set by Saint Francis of Assisi. Saint Francis founded this religious group of men in the early 1200s. To become a member, one had to vow never to marry and to live in poverty and in total obedience to God. While studying with these learned, religious men, Miguel José admired them and decided that he

▲
Fray Serra was the first president of the California missions. His robe was made of plain gray wool.

wanted to join the Franciscan brotherhood.

Serra entered a Franciscan monastery at age 16 and became a Franciscan friar two years later, in 1731. One tradition of this Catholic order was to rename oneself after a favorite Franciscan. Miguel José became Junípero, after a Franciscan who had been a close companion of Saint Francis.

18

Serra spent the next several years at another monastery, first as a student to become a Catholic priest, and later as a teacher.

A New Opportunity

In 1749, Catholic missionaries were needed in New Spain to convert the Indian people. Fray Serra and two former students of his, Francisco Palóu and Juan Crespí had heard of the Indians who lived in the New World. The friars were excited to join in the mission work, even though this meant they would probably never see their homeland again. The missionaries boarded a ship, which took them across the Atlantic Ocean to New Spain.

When they arrived in the port city of Veracruz, Mexico, the missionaries still had close to 269 miles (433 km) to reach their station in Veracruz. They spent about 14 days walking to reach the College of San Fernando in Mexico City.

The weather was extremely hot, and the wool robes the friars wore made it even hotter. Their open-toed sandals offered no protection from the sand which aggravated their feet. Yet, the friars never complained.

> Biographers estimate that Serra walked more than 24,000 miles (38,624 km) in California to establish and maintain the missions. That is more than Marco Polo's journey and the trek of Lewis and Clark combined!

As they journeyed, many mosquitoes and bugs bothered the travelers. One evening, an insect of some kind bit Fray Serra on the left foot, giving him an infection.

Even though the pain from the infection in Serra's leg became unbearable, he convinced his travelmates that he was well enough to continue their journey. The pain in his leg never ceased and even caused him to limp for the rest of his life. Once in Mexico City, Serra spent 17 years working for the College of San Fernando.

Baja California and Alta California

In 1767, Fray Serra was chosen to go to what is today northwestern Mexico, a part of the Baja Peninsula, to supervise the 15 existing Spanish missions. Serra worked hard to please the Franciscan friars who ran each individual mission. A year later, Spain decided to strengthen its claim to Alta California. This event changed Fray Serra's life.

▲
The first military governor of California, Gaspár de Portolá, led the expedition to establish settlements in Alta California.

The viceroy of New Spain was eager to explore and settle the land of Alta California. He appointed Gaspár de Portolá to lead a group to establish settlements there. Portolá sent three ships and two walking expeditions to San Diego. One ship was lost at sea. Fray Junípero Serra accompanied Portolá on one of the land groups, which left from New Spain in March 1769. On July 16, 1769, Fray Serra founded California's first mission, Mission San Diego de Alcalá. This was the first permanent European settlement in California.

Not only was Serra involved in the planning of the missions along the coast of California, but he was also the mission president in charge of all the missions. Two friars were appointed to each mission and were responsible for bringing the California Indians to the mission and baptizing them. Baptism is a ritual that involves immersing a person in water and having him or her commit to the Christian faith. Once baptized, the missionaries referred to the Christian Indians as neophytes. This translates to "newly planted," but the missionaries used it to mean newly converted. The missionaries also worked hard to teach the neophytes trades that would help bring in money for the mission. Serra made sure that the individual friars for each mission were doing their jobs.

The missions formed a chain along the Pacific Coast. The missions shown in light purple came after Mission Santa Bárbara, the ones in black came before. ▶

San Francisco Solano
San Rafael Arcángel
San Francisco de Asís
San José
Santa Clara de Asís
Santa Cruz
San Juan Bautista
San Carlos Borromeo de Carmelo
Nuestra Señora de la Soledad
San Antonio de Padua
San Miguel Arcángel
San Luis Obispo de Tolosa
La Purísima Concepción
Santa Inés
Santa Bárbara
San Buenaventura
San Fernando Rey de España
San Gabriel Arcángel
San Juan Capistrano
San Luis Rey de Francia
San Diego de Alcalá

▲

Mission Santa Barbara had an elaborate irrigation system that included several fountains.

As Serra and his companions planned new mission sites, they looked for areas with plenty of fresh water, fertile soil for planting crops and feeding livestock, and a supply of wood for building mission structures and furniture. Most important, the mission had to be in an area where there were many Indians.

22

Fray Fermín Francisco de Lasuén

When Serra died in 1784, his biographer and former student, Fray Palóu, became the mission president for one year. After that Fray Fermín Francisco de Lasuén took over the work and established nine more missions in 18 years. Lasuén came to New Spain from Spain in 1761, about 12 years after his mentor and friend, Fray Serra. He worked in the Baja California missions before going to serve as a missionary at Mission San Diego de Alcalá.

Under Lasuén's guidance as mission president, the total number of baptisms throughout the mission chain increased from 7,000 to 37,000, and the number of neophytes living at the missions rose from 5,000 to 18,000.

▲

Mission Santa Bárbara was the first mission to be established under the leadership of Fray Fermín Lasuén, second president of the Alta California missions.

Founding and Building Mission Santa Bárbara

The Beginning of Santa Bárbara

Fray Serra founded nine missions and had chosen the site for the 10th, Mission Santa Bárbara, near the Chumash village of Siujtu.

Before they could begin building, however, Governor Neve, who was in charge of the California territory, had to give his approval. Serra sent a letter asking for permission to found Mission Santa Bárbara in April of 1782. Neve, who lived in New Spain, would not allow any more missions to be built. He believed more missions would give too much power to the missionaries.

It wasn't until 1786, when another governor, Governor Fages, had been appointed, that Mission Santa Bárbara was finally founded. Fray Lasuén held the first founding ceremony on December 4, 1786. A second ceremony was held two weeks later on December 16, so Governor Fages could attend.

Right after the February and March rainy season in 1787, construction on the first Santa Bárbara mission buildings began. The Chumash Indians were incredibly helpful in the building of the mission.

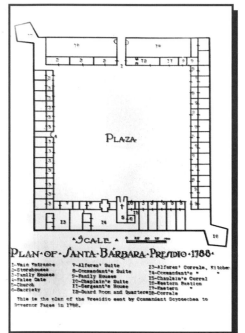

The Santa Barbara presidio was founded on May 18, 1782. This plan, or drawing, was made later, in 1788.

The neophytes at Mission Santa Bárbara helped to build the church and other mission buildings under the guidance of the friars. ▶

▲
The friars and Native Americans had different ideas about work. Sometimes this led to conflict and the Native Americans were often unhappy.

Building a Mission

The first buildings were constructed with logs. In 1789, an adobe church was built. Five years later, when the mission population outgrew its adobe building, a larger adobe church was built. In 1812, the third Santa Bárbara church was damaged in an earthquake, and the missionaries decided to construct a stone church. Not only would it be sturdier, but sandstone was also plentiful in the area.

In 1815, under the direction of Fray Antonio Ripoll, a new church was started. It was designed after a Roman building built before the birth of Christ. The church was completed in 1820 and stood unchanged for more than 100 years. Throughout most of the mission period, additional houses for neophytes were built every year. By 1834, there were more than 200 small adobe homes that made up the neophyte village.

Other buildings were built around the church, forming a square with an open area in the middle. This was called a

▲
These tools were brought from Mexico and Spain and were used to build the mission.

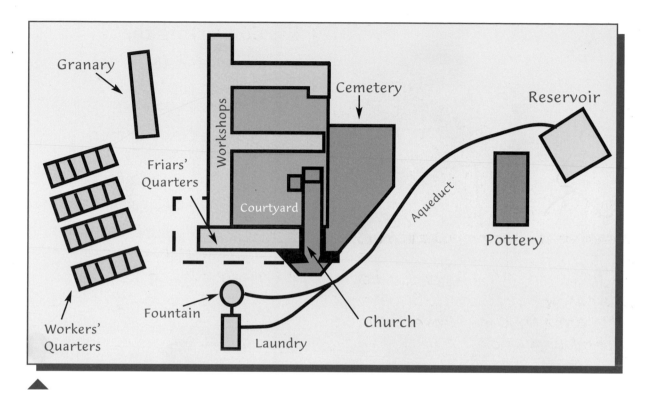

This is the layout of Mission Santa Bárbara.

quadrangle. Workshops were built where men could do hide tanning or shoemaking, and women could weave and make soap and candles. Unmarried women were grouped together in a large room called a *monjerío*. Each night the *monjerío* was locked to keep the women from leaving and to prevent unwelcome guests from sneaking in. The missionaries' quarters and a kitchen and dining area were also part of the quadrangle.

Converting the Chumash Indians

With shelter and protection provided, not to mention plenty of food offered by the missionaries, Mission Santa Bárbara was becoming an inviting place for some Indians. As the Chumash became comfortable at the mission site, the missionaries encouraged them to be baptized into the Christian faith. The missionaries tried to get the Indians interested in Christianity by playing beautiful music and holding lovely ceremonies. The Indians had enjoyed dance and music in their own religion. Once the Chumash were baptized, they were not

This picture hangs at the mission. It shows a Chumash Indian in his native dress. The Spanish didn't like nudity and made the neophytes wear clothes.

▲

The friars taught some neophytes how to play European instruments.

allowed to practice any previous religion they may have had.

As soon as the Indians became neophytes, the Spanish gave them clothes since nudity was not acceptable to the Europeans. Once a year, men were given a new pair of pants and women received a blouse and skirt.

29

At Mission Santa Bárbara, the friars encouraged the Indians to be baptized by allowing them to stay in their own villages. However, in the early 1800s, missionaries found that some neophytes had built altars to the gods their people had worshiped for centuries. The Franciscan friars began to enforce the rule that all neophytes had to live at the mission and were only allowed to make occasional visits to their old villages. The neophytes were also required to attend church twice daily and work at a given task every day. Some Indians did not like the many rules that were imposed on them by the missionaries.

Today we realize that the mission system violated the civil rights of many California Indians. We understand that it is not fair for a country to colonize land that belongs to another people. During the mission period, the Spanish missionaries and soldiers thought they were bringing a new and better way of life to the California Indians. Today it is clear that no group of people should be forced to accept the culture of another people or have to give up their own cultural and religious values and traditions.

This statue of Saint Bárbara is displayed inside the mission. Only five of the 21 California missions were named after women. These included Santa Inés, La Purísima Concepción, Santa Bárbara, Nuestra Señora de la Soledad, and Santa Clara de Asís. Saint Bárbara was a young girl who was supposedly beheaded by her father for following the Christian faith.

Daily Life for the Chumash Neophytes

The Chumash neophytes' daily routine varied little from day to day. The ringing of the bells set everyone's schedule at the Santa Bárbara mission, as well as the other missions. Every mission had at least two bells. One bell rang when it was time to pray or have devotions, while the other bell rang for work, mealtimes, and rest.

The Chumash Indians had never lived such a structured lifestyle. They were used to working when they needed to work and sleeping when they were tired. The missions changed that way of life.

▲ *Mission Santa Bárbara's* **campanario,** *or bell tower*

A day for the neophyte always started at sunrise, when everyone went to the church to pray and sing. Mass was in Latin and individual prayers were in the Chumash language. An hour later, the bell rang for breakfast. At 7:00 A.M., the neophytes went to do their work. They ate their afternoon meal and took a *siesta*, or a nap, at around noon. Two hours later, everyone returned to work. At 5:00 P.M., the Chumash again attended the mission church, listening to the missionaries' prayers and Bible lessons. After an hour of church, supper was held for all, followed by free time. A bell rang at 8:00 P.M. for women to go to bed. The final bell of the day rang at 9:00 P.M., signaling bedtime for the men.

◀ *Daily life at the mission was governed by the ringing of bells. Bells rang to signal important events throughout the day.*

33

The lavandería *was used to wash clothes.*

Neophytes labored at different assigned tasks in order to keep the mission running. They learned how to weave, farm, tan leather, and make tools. They learned these trades so that they could one day run the mission independently, without help from the friars.

Many of the men were busy with the construction of Mission Santa Bárbara. Every year more homes were built to fill the needs of the growing neophyte population. Workers were required to make 40 adobe bricks a day. Much time was also devoted to establishing and maintaining an extensive water system.

As with many other missions, Mission Santa Bárbara had an irrigation system built on its grounds. In 1806, a dam, reservoir, and aqueduct were built to carry water from a creek directly behind the mission. In all, Mission Santa Bárbara had two dams, two reservoirs, a filter house, a mill, a fountain, a *lavandería* or washing area, and several water channels that carried water to the fields, orchards, *monjerío*, and to the mission itself.

Crops were a main source of income for the missions, but not all missions were fortunate enough to have the proper conditions for

▲

Like most missions, Santa Bárbara cultivated grapevines that originally came from Mexico and Spain.

growing grapevines. Mission Santa Bárbara had at least three vineyards, with close to 6,000 vines. In addition about 100 fruit trees were planted.

The water system, which was started in 1806, was so well built that parts of it were still used by the city of Santa Barbara until a few years ago.

35

Many of the crops, such as corn and wheat, were ground down and used for flour or porridge. The Chumash had been grinding down seeds with stone mortars long before they met the Spaniards. Eventually iron mills were introduced to the mission, which supposedly allowed four women to grind down the same amount of food as it took 100 women to do with the stone mortars.

Even though Chumash women had woven baskets from grass for centuries, they had never woven cloth, particularly out of wool from sheep. In 1787, Mission Santa Bárbara started with 27 sheep. By 1803, it had 11,221 sheep on its grounds. The cloth-weaving trade became an important one for the mission because the neophytes could use what they needed and sell the extras. During the peak weaving months, from March to October, the weavers made 10 yards (9.14 m) of wool cloth a day. They were paid with glass beads or wheat for each additional

This weaving exhibit is on display at the Mission Santa Bárbara museum.

36

10 yards (9.14 m) they made. Those who made blankets had to weave three a day, while each spinner spun a pound of yarn every day.

As the years passed, and the mission population leveled out, many neophytes were given the task of recruiting other California Indians into the mission system. They were sent out to their old villages, as well as to other tribal villages miles away, and ordered to bring back more Indians, who were often brought against their will. We know today that the Indians' choices were not respected and that their freedom was unjustly trespassed upon under the mission system.

The meals at Mission Santa Bárbara were basically the same day after day. For breakfast and dinner, the neophytes received *atole*, which was similar to oatmeal. Their main meal of the day was *pozole*, a type of stew with meat and vegetables. They also sometimes received fruit that was in season at the time, and the Indians were free to eat whatever they picked in the nearby area. Recent archaeological findings also show that the Chumash did continue to hunt and gather traditional foods at Mission Santa Bárbara.

Daily Life for the Missionaries and Soldiers

Two missionaries headed Mission Santa Bárbara. Several Spanish soldiers worked for them, protecting the missions from outside attack and punishing disobedient neophytes.

It was the Catholic friars' responsibility to educate the neophytes in their religion. They led the young children in studies each morning and afternoon while the adults worked. They also taught the Spanish language to some of the young Chumash children, who eventually became interpreters between the missionaries and the Indians.

While the friars never gained financially from the Indians' work, the missionaries did have to make sure the neophytes learned a trade. The goods the mission produced kept it financially strong. If the mission lost its income, then the missionaries would not have the means to continue their work. This meant they were sometimes forced to have the soldiers discipline those neophytes who did not do their jobs. The soldiers were also the ones to retrieve neophytes who tried to escape back to their villages. Those Chumash who longed for their old way of life often had to deal with beatings or even periods of being jailed or locked in shackles.

The neophytes who worked hard to please the missionaries were free from harm and punishment. The younger Indians who had been raised in the mission system knew of no other life. However, they learned of their people's past life of freedom from the older neophytes, their elders who longed for these old ways. As the years passed, discontent at the mission continued to grow, especially since the mission lands the Indians took care of were never given back to them.

The missionaries taught neophytes about Christianity and Spanish culture. ▶

Troubles at Mission Santa Bárbara

All 21 of the California missions had problems. In its peaceful setting overlooking the Pacific Ocean, Mission Santa Bárbara seemed, for a while, to be above any strife. Its main problems did not involve fires and floods, which plagued many of the other missions. Instead the troubles at Mission Santa Bárbara were mostly civil problems.

The Rebellion of 1824

As the years passed at the missions, neophytes grew more and more discontented. They missed their families and the lifestyle their people had experienced for centuries. They missed the freedom they had once had to practice their own religion, to hunt and gather their food, and to live in their villages. The Indians were also very distraught because so many of their people had died from diseases brought by the Spaniards.

Many Chumash neophytes ran away from Mission Santa Bárbara. Noticing that many Chumash tried to return to their villages, the missionaries began to allow friends and family to visit mission neophytes. Unfortunately this was a rather weak gesture and one probably made too late.

In February 1824, a revolt by neophytes started at Mission Santa Inés and then swept to Mission La Purísima Concepción. These two missions were not far from Mission Santa Bárbara. The revolt was started because a soldier beat an Indian neophyte. The neophytes at Mission Santa Bárbara, persuaded to follow the example of the rebellious California Indians of Santa Inés and La Purísima Concepción, decided to start their own revolt. It was only a matter of days before Mission Santa Bárbara was in turmoil. The revolt at Santa Bárbara

◀ *Fray Ripoll pleaded for the return of the Chumash during the Rebellion of 1824.*

Andres Sagimomatsse was one of the Chumash leaders of the Revolt of 1824.

wasn't as bad as at the other two missions, but soldiers from the *presidio* threatened the Indians.

One of the Indian leaders at Mission Santa Bárbara, Andres Sagimomatsse, took the Indian women and children from the mission and hid them in the hills where they would be safe. Then he and several other men grabbed some weapons, ready to attack the Spanish soldiers from the Purísima *presidio* who were marching toward Mission Santa Bárbara. In the small battle, several Chumash and some Spanish travelers were killed.

Sagimomatsse and other Chumash raced to the hills to find other California Indians who would help in the fight. They were never able to organize a full-scale rebellion, and many ended up returning to the mission because they had nowhere else to go.

Disease

The biggest problem at Mission Santa Bárbara, and every other California mission, was the threat of disease for the Indians. When the Spanish came over from Europe, they brought with them illnesses, such as measles, smallpox, pneumonia, mumps, and diphtheria.

Friars at Mission Santa Bárbara reported that the mission had enough medicine, which was used frequently by both neophytes and the missionaries. Despite the healing methods the friars tried to use, thousands of Indians died. Since they had never been exposed to the European illnesses, their bodies had no immunity to these diseases. Due to these deaths, the California Indian population declined drastically.

▲
Stone carvings of skulls and crossbones decorate the door of the mission church that leads to the cemetery. Originally, real human skulls and bones hung here.

The Secularization of the Missions

Up until the 1820s, the missions, including the land the missions were built on, were part of New Spain. Spain had settled much of its empire by developing the mission system.

In 1821, New Spain won a war against Spain to separate itself from the rule of the Spanish king and queen. New Spain became an independent country and was renamed Mexico.

The newly founded Mexican government wanted the rich lands of Alta California for itself. They planned to send more Mexican settlers north to California to settle more of the land, which would make Mexico stronger. The Mexican government planned to secularize the missions, which means to change from religious to political rule. They planned to take some land for themselves and turn most of it over to the Indians. This meant taking the missions away from the Franciscan friars.

The missionaries, who would lose all they had worked for over the past several years, were against secularization. The Spanish missionaries wanted to convert the Indians to Christianity and teach them to be independent inhabitants of the missions. They did not think the neophytes were ready to survive on their own. The friars had changed the Chumash culture. The Chumash, who had lived independently and undisturbed for centuries, had become dependent on the mission system.

From 1823 to 1836, the neophyte population at Mission Santa Bárbara gradually decreased from 962 to 481 individuals. While Mexico's original intention of secularization was to turn all the mission lands over to the Indians, this did not end up happening. When José Figueroa was appointed governor of the California territory, he

Mission Santa Bárbara is the only mission which has been served continuously by the Franciscan friars. ▶

▲

Parts of the mission deteriorated after secularization.

secularized the missions without permission from the Mexican government. Governor Figueroa never planned to turn the valuable land over to the Indians. He expected the Indians to continue working in the mission fields to make goods to sell in order to pay the salaries of the administrators under the governor.

Mission Santa Bárbara was secularized in 1834, but it remained occupied by Fray Narciso Duran, the last of the mission presidents. Fray Duran was again placed in charge of the Indians in 1839 due to the deterioration of Mission Santa Bárbara after the secularization. Several years later, Alta California's first bishop came to live at the beautiful mission. With these influential men on the Santa Bárbara premises, the Mexican government left the mission alone.

In 1846, the two men died within months of each other, and Pio Pico, the Mexican governor at that time, quickly took over the lands to sell and make a profit for himself. He sold the land to two Mexican farmers, Nicholas Den and Daniel Hill. The resident Indians were then forced to leave the mission land or to stay and work for the new owners.

▲
Among those buried beneath the church floor of Mission Santa Bárbara is Governor José Figueroa.

There were still other changes to come. In the late 1840s, gold was found near the Sacramento River. People from all over the United States traveled to California hoping to find gold. They were known as the "forty-niners." This new group of people wanted California to be part of the United States. When California became the 31st state, the sale Pio Pico made was invalidated. Mission Santa Barbara was given to the Catholic Church, this time by the U.S. government.

The Tradition Continues

Mission Santa Bárbara is known as the Queen of the Missions for its ideal location in the hills overlooking the ocean and, today, the city of Santa Barbara.

If you take a walk around the grounds of Mission Santa Bárbara, you may find yourself back in time almost 200 years. You may even see Franciscan friars walking about, wearing traditional woolen robes gathered at the waist with a white piece of cord. Approximately 30 friars live at the mission today.

During a 1925 earthquake, the mission was severely damaged. It was eventually repaired. The mission has retained its original appearance, and most of the tile floors are original.

The Santa Bárbara mission is one of only four missions now under the control of the Franciscans (the other missions are San Luis Rey de Francia, San Antonio de Padua, and San Miguel Arcángel). There are about 800 families in the Santa Bárbara church's membership. Services are held daily.

A re-creation of a friar's bedroom at the mission

A walk through the museum will show rooms re-created from the mission period. For instance in a friar's bedroom you can see the sparse furnishings, including the bed, which is an animal skin pulled tight across a bed frame. In the kitchen, a large stone fireplace takes

◀ *This is Mission Santa Bárbara today.*

Make Your Own Model
Mission Santa Bárbara

To make your own model of Mission Santa Bárbara, you will need:

foamcore board	scissors
ruler	glue
paint (red, white, tan)	Popsicle sticks
cardboard	sand

Directions

Step 1: Cut a 20″ x 20″ (50.8 x 50.8 cm) piece of foamcore for the base of your mission. Mix tan paint with sand for texture, and paint the base with this mixture.

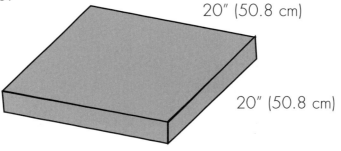

20″ (50.8 cm)

20″ (50.8 cm)

Adult supervision is recommended.

The Tradition Continues

Mission Santa Bárbara is known as the Queen of the Missions for its ideal location in the hills overlooking the ocean and, today, the city of Santa Barbara.

If you take a walk around the grounds of Mission Santa Bárbara, you may find yourself back in time almost 200 years. You may even see Franciscan friars walking about, wearing traditional woolen robes gathered at the waist with a white piece of cord. Approximately 30 friars live at the mission today.

During a 1925 earthquake, the mission was severely damaged. It was eventually repaired. The mission has retained its original appearance, and most of the tile floors are original.

The Santa Bárbara mission is one of only four missions now under the control of the Franciscans (the other missions are San Luis Rey de Francia, San Antonio de Padua, and San Miguel Arcángel). There are about 800 families in the Santa Bárbara church's membership. Services are held daily.

▲
A re-creation of a friar's bedroom at the mission

A walk through the museum will show rooms re-created from the mission period. For instance in a friar's bedroom you can see the sparse furnishings, including the bed, which is an animal skin pulled tight across a bed frame. In the kitchen, a large stone fireplace takes

◀ *This is Mission Santa Bárbara today.*

The mission cemetery has many types of grave markers.

up much of the room, as does a table used for preparing meals of *atole* and *pozole*.

Attached to the museum and church is the cemetery. Grave markers range from unnamed wooden crosses to fancy, huge marble mausoleums that hold entire families. In all, there are more than 4,000 Indians buried there. (The young girl whose life story is told in *Island of the Blue Dolphins*, the award-winning book by Scott O'Dell, was also buried there in an unmarked spot in 1853.)

All the people who lived at Mission Santa Bárbara, and the other missions, helped to make California the state it is today. The Spanish missionaries and soldiers introduced farming to the California Indians. Today California farms are an important food source for the United States. The Chumash and other Indian tribes who built the missions left valuable paintings,

This is the main altar of the church at Mission Santa Bárbara.

baskets, pottery, and other goods that give us a sense of life in the 1700s and 1800s.

If you visit Mission Santa Bárbara, you will see the large fountain that stands in front of the mission. Since 1808, the fountain has stored water for the wash basin below it. Today this fountain is a beautiful reminder of civilizations past.

The mission is home to the Santa Bárbara Mission Archives, an extensive selection of books, documents, and articles on all the California missions. It includes Fray Serra's diary, as well as letters from Fray Serra to his friends Fray Lasuén, Fray Palóu, and Fray Crespí.

▲

This fountain sits in front of Mission Santa Bárbara.

Make Your Own Model
Mission Santa Bárbara

To make your own model of Mission Santa Bárbara, you will need:

foamcore board	scissors
ruler	glue
paint (red, white, tan)	Popsicle sticks
cardboard	sand

Directions

Step 1: Cut a 20" x 20" (50.8 x 50.8 cm) piece of foamcore for the base of your mission. Mix tan paint with sand for texture, and paint the base with this mixture.

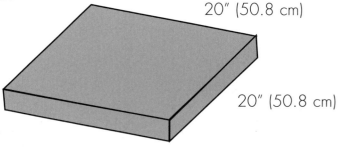

20" (50.8 cm)

20" (50.8 cm)

Adult supervision is recommended.

Step 2: Cut a 30" x 11" (76.2 x 27.9 cm) piece of cardboard for the church. On both sides, cut lightly into the cardboard three 3" (7.6 cm) sections.

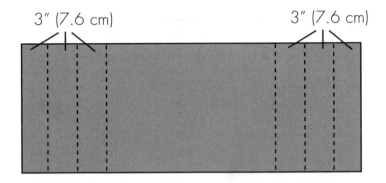

3" (7.6 cm)   3" (7.6 cm)

Step 3: In the center of the top edge of the board, cut out a 6" x 5" (15.2 x 12.7 cm) rectangle.

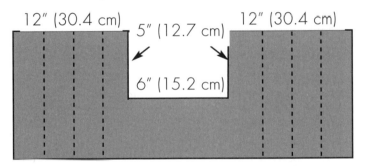

12" (30.4 cm)   5" (12.7 cm)   12" (30.4 cm)

6" (15.2 cm)

Step 4: Cut two arched windows at the top of each 3" (7.6 cm) section. Cut two arched windows on either side of the cut-out square. Cut a door in the center of the bottom edge.

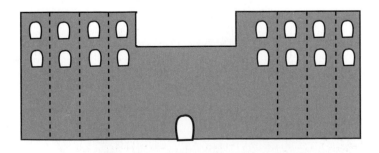

Step 5: Fold the cardboard to form the bell towers and the front of the church.

Step 6: Cut two 3" x 3" (7.6 x 7.6 cm) squares of cardboard. Glue to top of the bell towers. Add a dome made of clay to each.

 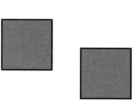

Step 7: For the back of the church, cut two walls that measure 4" x 6" (10.2 x 15.2 cm). Cut one square (for the rear wall) that measures 6" x 6" (15.2 x15.2).

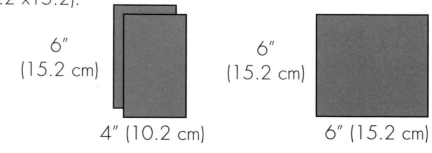

6"
(15.2 cm)

6"
(15.2 cm)

4" (10.2 cm)

6" (15.2 cm)

54

Step 8: To make the pointed roof of the church, cut two triangles that are 6" (15.2 cm) wide and 3" (7.6 cm) at the peak. Glue one to the top edge of the back wall and one between the bell towers.

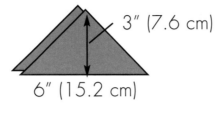

3" (7.6 cm)

6" (15.2 cm)

Step 9: Paint Popsicle sticks red and glue to the triangle to make the tiled roof.

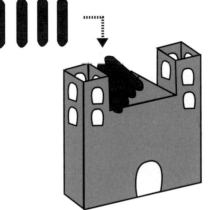

Step 10: To make the friars' quarters, cut two 11" x 5" (27.9 x 12.7 cm) cardboard rectangles to make the front and back walls.

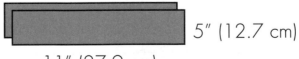

5" (12.7 cm)

11" (27.9 cm)

Step 11: Cut ten arched doors and a small window above each door in one of the walls.

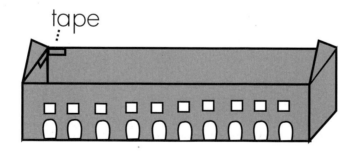

Step 12: Cut two 4" x 6.5" (10.2 x 16.5 cm) pieces of cardboard for the end walls of the friars' quarters. Then cut off the corners.

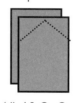

6.5" (16.5 cm)

4" (10.2 cm)

Step 13: Put the front, back, and end walls of the friars' quarters together, and tape the inside corners.

tape

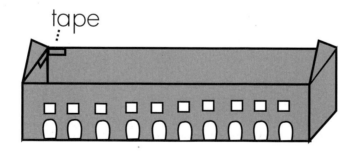

Step 14: To make the roof of the friars' quarters, cut a 11" x 5" (27.9 x 12.5 cm) piece of cardboard and bend it lengthwise down the middle. Glue the roof to the top of the building.

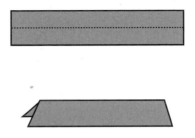

Step 15: Glue three thin strips of cardboard to each side of the door. Mix white paint with sand. Paint the mission with this mixture. Add trees and grass to the mission grounds.

*Use the above mission as a reference for building your mission.

Important Dates in Mission History

1492	Christopher Columbus reaches the West Indies
1542	Cabrillo's expedition to California
1602	Sebastian Vizcaíno sails to California
1713	Fray Junípero Serra is born
1769	Founding of San Diego de Alcalá
1770	Founding of San Carlos Borromeo de Carmelo
1771	Founding of San Antonio de Padua and San Gabriel Arcángel
1772	Founding of San Luis Obispo de Tolosa
1775–76	Founding of San Juan Capistrano
1776	Founding of San Francisco de Asís
1776	Declaration of Independence is signed
1777	Founding of Santa Clara de Asís
1782	Founding of San Buenaventura
1784	Fray Serra dies
1786	**Founding of Santa Bárbara**
1787	Founding of La Purísima Concepción
1791	Founding of Santa Cruz and Nuestra Señora de la Soledad
1797	Founding of San José, San Juan Bautista, San Miguel Arcángel, and San Fernando Rey de España
1798	Founding of San Luis Rey de Francia
1804	Founding of Santa Inés
1817	Founding of San Rafael Arcángel
1823	Founding of San Francisco Solano
1848	Gold found in northern California
1850	California becomes the 31st state

Glossary

adobe (uh-DOH-bee) Sun-dried bricks made of straw, mud, and sometimes manure.

baptism (BAP-tih-zum) A ceremony performed when someone accepts the Christian faith.

Catholicism (kuh-THAH-lih-sih-zum) The faith or practice of Catholic Christianity, which includes following the spiritual leadership of priests headed by the pope.

Christianity (kris-chee-A-nih-tee) A religion based on the teachings of Jesus Christ and the Bible, practiced by Eastern, Roman Catholic, and Protestant groups.

colonize (KAH-luh-nyz) To claim and take control of land to establish a colony.

convert (kun-VURT) To change from belief in one religion to belief in another religion.

Franciscan (fran-SIS-kin) A communal Roman Catholic order of friars, or "brothers" who follow the teachings and example of Saint Francis of Assisi.

friar (FRY-ur) A brother in a communal religious order. Friars also can be priests.

irrigation (eer-ih-GAY-shun) To supply with water.

livestock (LYV-stohk) Farm animals kept for use or profit.

Mass (MAS) A Christian religious ceremony.

mausoleum (maw-sah-LEE-um) A large tomb that is above ground.

missionary (MIH-shun-ayr-ee) A person who teaches his or her religion to people with different beliefs.

mission president (MIH-shun PREH-zih-dent) A person who was in charge of a group of missions in a particular area. Frays Serra, Lasuén, and Duran all served as mission presidents.

neophyte (NEE-uh-fyt) The name for the American Indians once baptized to the Christian faith.

presidio (preh-SIH-dee-oh) A Spanish military fort.

quarters (KWOR-turz) Rooms where someone lives.

secularization (seh-kyoo-luh-rih-ZAY-shun) A process by which the mission lands were made to be nonreligious.

shaman (SHAH-min) A religious and spiritual leader who heals the sick through medicine and ritual.

tanning (TA-ning) Taking animal skins and making them into leather that can be used.

tule (TOO-lee) Reeds used by the Indians to make houses and boats.

viceroy (VYS-roy) A governor who rules and acts as the representative of the king.

villages (VIH-lih-jiz) Original communities where American Indians lived before the arrival of the Spanish.

60

Pronunciation Guide

atole (ah-TOH-lay)

campanario (kam-pah-NAH-ree-oh)

fray (FRAY)

lavandería (lah-ban-deh-REE-ah)

monjerío (mohn-hay-REE-oh)

pozole (poh-SOH-lay)

siesta (see-EHS-tah)

temescal (TEH-mes-kal)

tomol (TOH-mul)

Resources

If you would like to learn more about the California missions, check out these books, videos, and Web sites:

Books
Behrens, June. *Missions of the Central Coast.* Minneapolis, MN: Lerner
   Publications Company, 1996.
Genet, Donna. *Father Junípero Serra: Founder of the California
   Missions.* Springfield, NJ: Enslow Publishers, 1996.
Keyworth, C. L. *The First Americans: California Indians.* New York:
   Facts on File, 1991.

Videos
Missions of California: *Father Junípero Serra.* Produced by Chip Taylor
   Productions. Should be available in your library. You can also order
   the tape by calling 1-800-876-CHIP.

Web Sites
Due to the changing nature of Internet links, PowerKids Press has
developed an online list of Web sites related to the subject of this book
This site is updated regularly. Please use this link to access the list:
www.powerkidslinks.com/moca/msantaba/

Museums
Here are two places in the Santa Barbara area you might want to visit,
along with their phone numbers.

Mission Santa Bárbara
2201 Laguna Street
Santa Barbara, CA 93105
805/682-4713

The Santa Barbara Museum of Art
2559 Puesta del Sol
Santa Barbara, CA 93105
805/963-4364

Index